SUSTAINABLE LIVING

HARRIET BRUNDLE

PROTECTING OUR
PLANET

©2018
Book Life
King's Lynn
Norfolk PE30 4LS

ISBN: 978-1-78637-265-9

Written by:
Harriet Brundle

Edited by:
Kirsty Holmes

Designed by:
Gareth Liddington

A catalogue record for this book
is available from the British Library.

Photocredits: Abbreviations: l-left, r-right, b-bottom, t-top, c-centre, m-middle. All images are courtesy of Shutterstock.com.

Covert – Volodymyr Kyrylyuk, Coverm – artjazz, Coverb – miroslav110, 1l – s-1s, 1r – FooTToo, 2 – wavebreakmedia, 3 – kpboonjit, 4 – Chinnapong, 5 – Sunny studio, 6 – Romolo Tavani, 7bg – Anan Kaewkhammul, 7br – oleandra, 8 – Mopic, 9 – Monkey Business Images, 10 – Rawpixel.com, 11 – Sappasit, 12 – ARIMAG, 13 – Aleksandr Ryabov, 14 – smereka, 15t – Kostiantyn Kravchenko, 15m – CPM PHOTO, 15b – Ildi Papp, 16 – OmiStudio, 17 – Africa Studio, 18 – Pawel Michalowski, 19 – Chinnapong, 20 – Soonthorn Wongsaita, 21 – Mimadeo, 22 – Hurst Photo, 23 – Stock-Asso, 24 – spwidoff.

Images are courtesy of Shutterstock.com. With thanks to Getty Images, Thinkstock Photo and iStockphoto.

CONTENTS

Words that look like **this** can be found in the glossary on page 24.

WHAT IS
SUSTAINABLE LIVING?

If something is 'sustainable' it means it is looked after so it can last a long time. Living in a sustainable way is all about making choices that help to look after our planet, so it can carry on **supporting** the people that live here now and in the future.

There are over seven billion people living on Earth. If each person made a small change to live in a more sustainable way, it would have a big impact!

WHY IS SUSTAINABLE LIVING IMPORTANT?

The things we need to live are called resources. Many of these are **limited**. Other types of resources, like wood from trees, must be replaced so we can use them in the future.

OIL

COAL

Coal and oil are found under the Earth's **surface**. They are used to make energy, which powers our cars and homes. These resources will run out in the future if we don't find more sustainable ways of doing

CARBON
FOOTPRINT

THE AMOUNT OF CARBON DIOXIDE YOU RELEASE IS CALLED YOUR CARBON FOOTPRINT.

We use energy to power things we use, like cars and light bulbs. Most of our energy comes from burning **fossil fuels**, which releases **carbon dioxide**.

Carbon dioxide is harmful to the environment, so it is important that we all try to lower the amount we produce.

COULD YOU WALK OR RIDE YOUR BIKE TO SCHOOL?

RECYCLE

Recycling is when old **materials** we no longer need are turned into new ones. Lots of things can be recycled including paper, plastic and metal.

THIS SIGN MEANS SOMETHING CAN BE RECYCLED.

When we throw things away, they are usually burned or buried in the earth. If we can recycle materials, this does not have to happen. Recycling helps us to lower our carbon footprint.

REDUCE AND
REUSE

We can all try to live in a more sustainable way by reusing things, rather than buying more. When you go to the shops, take a bag with you, rather than asking for a new plastic one.

THIS MEANS FEWER PLASTIC BAGS WILL BE MADE, WHICH IS BETTER FOR THE ENVIRONMENT.

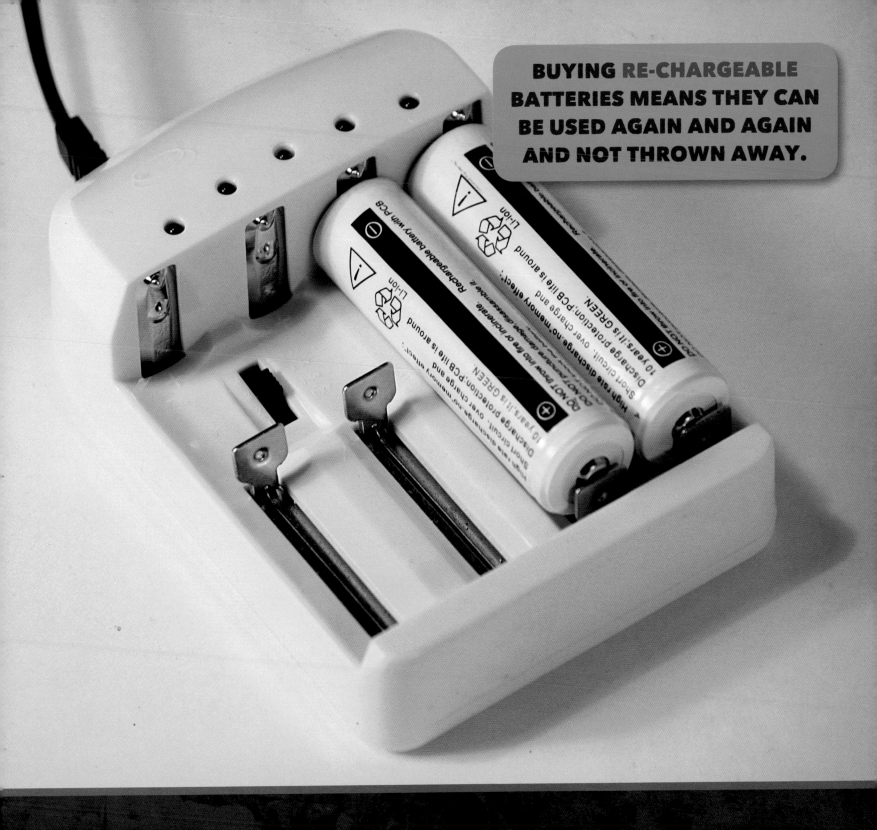

BUYING RE-CHARGEABLE BATTERIES MEANS THEY CAN BE USED AGAIN AND AGAIN AND NOT THROWN AWAY.

Reducing the amount we buy helps the environment. We must try to share with others and only buy things that we really need.

GROW YOUR OWN

Lots of the foods we eat are often moved from the place they are made or grown and taken to the shops by large lorries, which release carbon dioxide into the air.

TOMATOES

LETTUCES

BEANS

We can try to live more sustainably by growing some of our own food at home or at school. With an area of soil and some seeds, we can grow lots of different foods including tomatoes, lettuces and beans.

SAVING WATER

Every living thing needs water. We use water not only for drinking but also for washing, cooking and lots of other jobs every day. It takes time and energy to recycle water, so it is important we don't waste it.

There are lots of things you can do to help save water:

1. Turn off the tap while you are brushing your teeth.

2. Keep a jug of water in the fridge so you can have cold drinking water without running the tap for a long time.

3. If possible, try to have a short shower rather than a bath as showers use less water.

THINK LOCAL, ACT GLOBAL

One way to help live a more sustainable life is to remember the saying "Think Local – Act **Global**". This means we can all help to keep our planet healthy by taking big or small actions in our local area.

We can all make small changes to live more sustainably. We can use less water, grow our own food or use a bike instead of a car. Together we can help make a difference to the planet.

NEW TECHNOLOGIES

In the past, different types of **technology** have been used to try and help us live more sustainably. As we have learnt more about our planet and how to look after it, the technology we use has become much more **efficient**.

By using things that will never run out, like the wind, we can produce energy without harming the environment.

WIND TURBINES USE THE WIND TO PRODUCE ENERGY.

Low-energy light bulbs can be used at home. They use much less energy and last much longer than normal light bulbs.

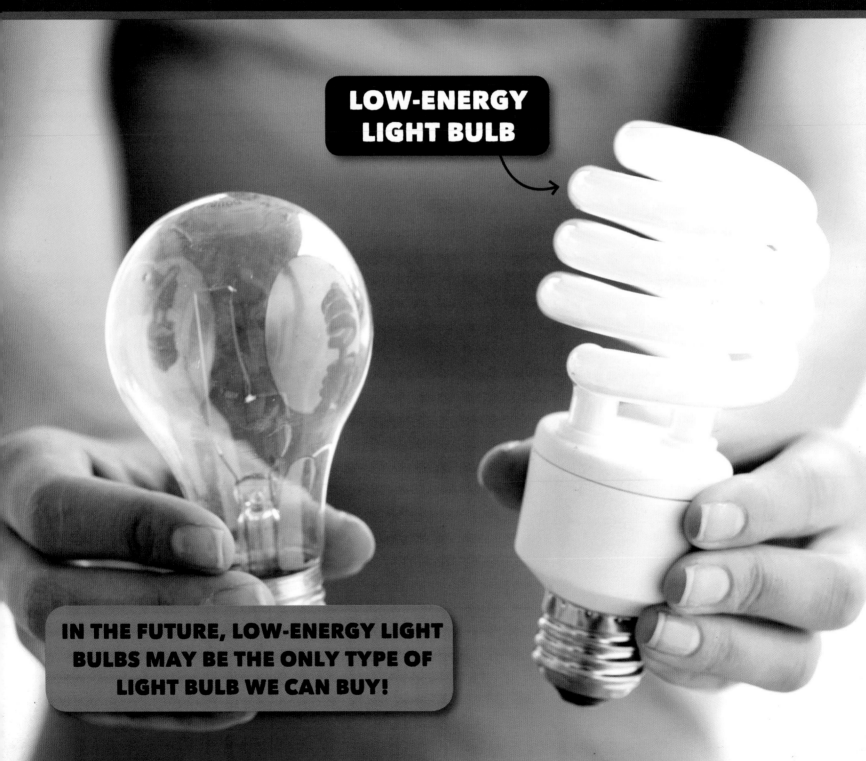

LOW-ENERGY LIGHT BULB

IN THE FUTURE, LOW-ENERGY LIGHT BULBS MAY BE THE ONLY TYPE OF LIGHT BULB WE CAN BUY!

WHAT DOES THE
FUTURE HOLD?

Countries all around the world are spending money on finding new ways to improve their carbon footprint and reduce harm to the environment. It is hoped that with these new technologies, we can all live a more sustainable lifestyle.

GLOSSARY AND INDEX

GLOSSARY

carbon dioxide   a natural, colourless gas that is found in the air
efficient   getting the most out of something in the best way possible
fossil fuels   fuels, such as coal, oil and gas, that formed millions of years ago
from the remains of animals and plants
global   relating to the whole world
limited   when something will run out because there is only so much of it
materials   the things from which other things are made
re-chargeable   something that is able to have its energy levels increased again
supporting   giving help to something or someone else
surface   the outer part of something
technology   things that have been made from scientific knowledge

INDEX